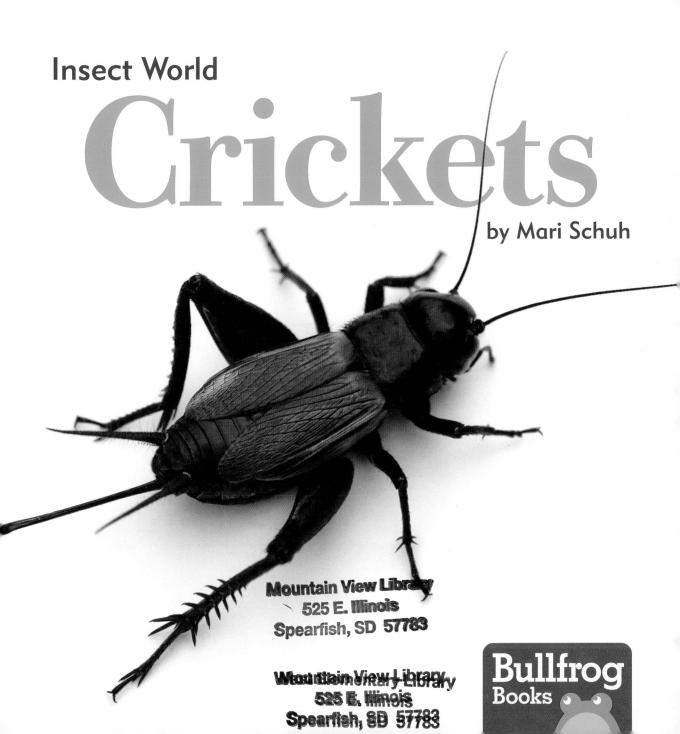

Insect World

Crickets

by Mari Schuh

Bullfrog
Books

Ideas for Parents and Teachers

Bullfrog Books let children practice nonfiction reading at the earliest reading levels. Repetition, familiar words, and photo labels support early readers.

Before Reading

- Discuss the cover photo. What does it tell them?
- Look at the picture glossary together. Read and discuss the words.

Read the Book

- "Walk" through the book and look at the photos. Let the child ask questions. Point out the photo labels.
- Read the book to the child, or have him or her read independently.

After Reading

- Prompt the child to think more. Ask: Have you ever seen a cricket? Where was it? What was it doing?

The author dedicates this book to Jadyn Friedrichs of Sioux City, Iowa.

Bullfrog Books are published by Jump!
5357 Penn Avenue South
Minneapolis, MN 55419
www.jumplibrary.com

Copyright © 2014 Jump! International copyright reserved in all countries. No part of this book may be reproduced in any form without written permission from the publisher.

Library of Congress Cataloging-in-
Schuh, Mari C., 1975-
  Crickets / by Mari Schuh.
    p. cm. -- (Insect world)
  Summary: "This photo-illustrated book for early readers tells why crickets chirp and briefly explains their life cycle. Includes picture glossary"--Provided by publisher.
  ISBN 978-1-62031-054-0 (hardcover : alk. paper)
  ISBN 978-1-62496-046-8 (ebook)
  1. Crickets--Juvenile literature. 2. Crickets--Life cycles--Juvenile literature. I. Title. II. Series: Schuh, Mari C., 1975- Insect world.
  QL508.G8 S38 2014
  595.7'26--dc23   2012039940

Series Editor   Rebecca Glaser
Book Designer   Ellen Huber
Photo Researcher Heather Dreisbach

Photo Credits: Alamy, 5, 9, 13; BigStock, 12; Corbis, 19, 23tr; Dreamstime, 1; Getty, 10–11, 17; iStock, 4; Science Source, 6–7, 20–21; Shutterstock, cover, 3, 8, 14–15, 16, 18, 22, 23tl, 23bl, 23br, 24

Printed in the United States of America at Corporate Graphics, North Mankato, Minnesota.
4-2013 / PO 1003

10 9 8 7 6 5 4 3 2 1

Table of Contents

A Cricket Song

Chirp. Chirp.
What do you hear?

A cricket
is chirping.

Why?

He wants
to mate.

How does he make sound?

wings

He rubs his wings.

He makes a song.
He sings at night.

Each kind of cricket
has his own song.

Females hear them.

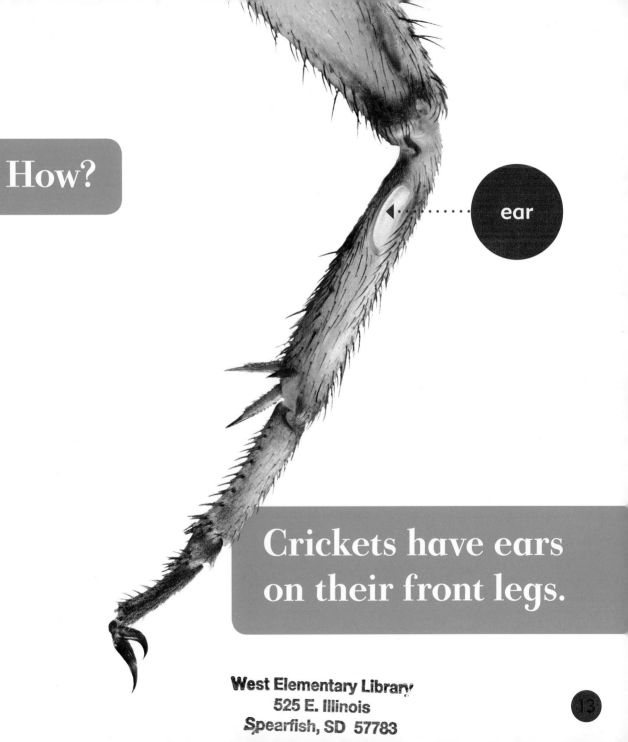

How?

ear

Crickets have ears
on their front legs.

13

Females find the males.
Males sing a new song.

They mate.

15

It is fall.

Females lay eggs.

The eggs
come out of
the egg tube.

Push, push.

egg

The eggs go into a plant.

egg
tube

17

Now it is spring.
Baby crickets are born.
They grow and grow.
They shed their skin.

old skin ·····▶

One day, they will make songs, too.

Chirp! Chirp!

Parts of a Cricket

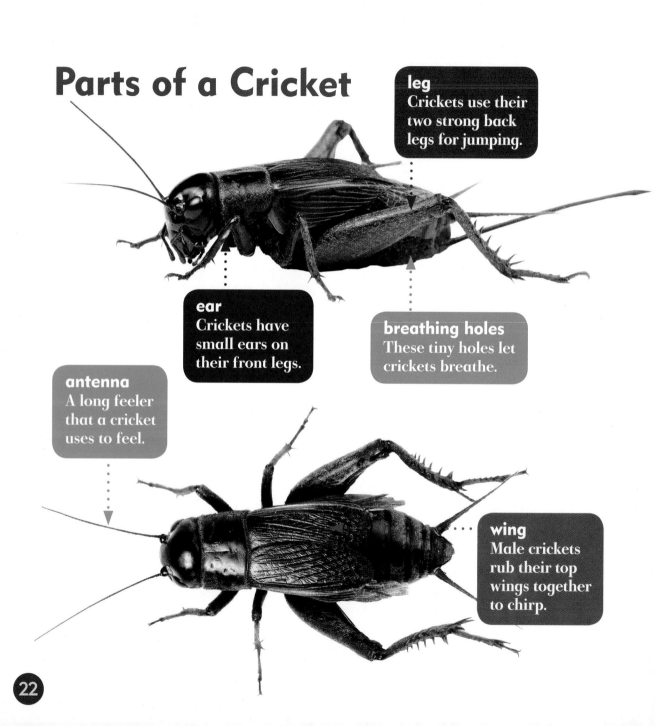

leg
Crickets use their two strong back legs for jumping.

ear
Crickets have small ears on their front legs.

breathing holes
These tiny holes let crickets breathe.

antenna
A long feeler that a cricket uses to feel.

wing
Male crickets rub their top wings together to chirp.

Picture Glossary

egg
A round or oval object that holds young animals before they are born.

mate
To join together to make young.

egg tube
A long part on the back of a female cricket that is used for laying eggs.

shed
To fall off or get rid of; young crickets shed their skin many times as they grow.

Index

To Learn More

Learning more is as easy as 1, 2, 3.

1) Go to www.factsurfer.com

2) Enter "cricket" into the search box.

3) Click the "Surf" button to see a list of websites.

With factsurfer.com, finding more information is just a click away.